STO

SF

P9-EEN-480

BEGINNING SCIENCE
WITH MR. WIZARD

BEGINNING SCIENCE
WITH MR. WIZARD

WATER

Don Herbert and Hy Ruchlis

ILLUSTRATED BY MEL HUNTER

DOUBLEDAY & COMPANY, INC.
GARDEN CITY, NEW YORK
1960

CO. SCHOOLS
C505184

Could you break a bottle with water?

Get a small bottle with a metal screw cap. Fill it to the brim with water. Screw the cap on tightly. Place the bottle in an empty food can. Put the can in the freezer compartment of the refrigerator.

In the morning you will find that the glass has shattered inside the can. It was broken by the freezing water.

Why did this happen?

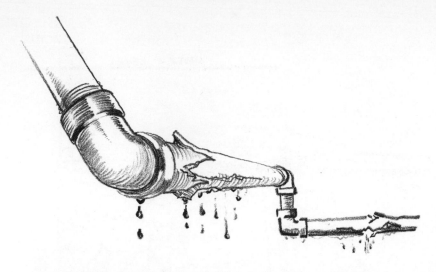

The bottle broke because of an unusual property of water. Most materials contract (become smaller) when they freeze or solidify. But water does the opposite. It actually expands (becomes larger) when it freezes. The force of this expansion is great enough to break iron water pipes on a very cold winter day.

This action by freezing water is very important in nature. It helps to break up rocks in the ground and change them into soil. Water gets into tiny cracks in the rocks when it rains. Then, in the winter, it freezes, expands, and cracks the rock.

In this manner the rocks on mountains are gradually broken up and worn down. This process, called erosion, can reduce the highest mountains to level plains after many millions of years.

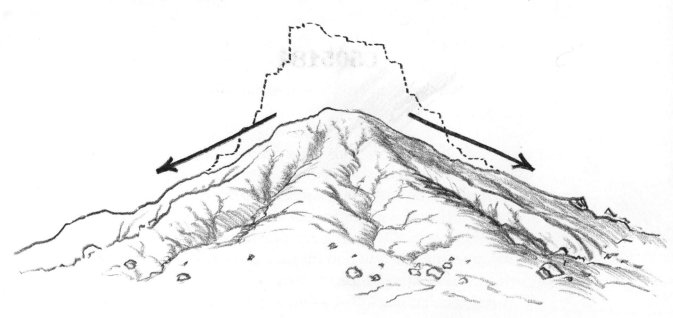

WATER LEVEL

In cold mountain areas, water falls from clouds in the form of snow. The snow packs into ice. Then the ice moves slowly down the sides of mountains as a glacier. This motion slowly wears away the mountain.

Icebergs are formed when the ends of glaciers reach the ocean and break off. These icebergs are very dangerous to ships. You can see why by floating ice cubes in a glass of water. About nine tenths of the ice cube will be under water, with only one tenth above water. If a ship gets too close to an iceberg, it can be damaged by the submerged ice.

As the iceberg melts, any rocks or soil it may have carried out to the sea will be deposited on the ocean bottom. The sides of the mountain end up at the bottom of the sea!

7

Water helps erode the land in still another way. Try this. Get a toy plastic pinwheel of the kind you use at the beach or park. Hold it under the faucet. Turn on a gentle stream of water. The pinwheel turns rapidly. Why?

When water moves fast it has a great deal of inertia and tends to keep going. It therefore exerts a force against anything that is in the way.

The faster the water moves, the more force it exerts. The water squirting out of the faucet moves fast enough to turn the pinwheel.

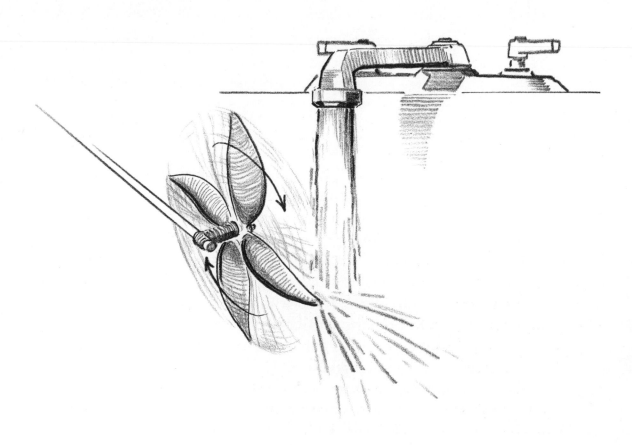

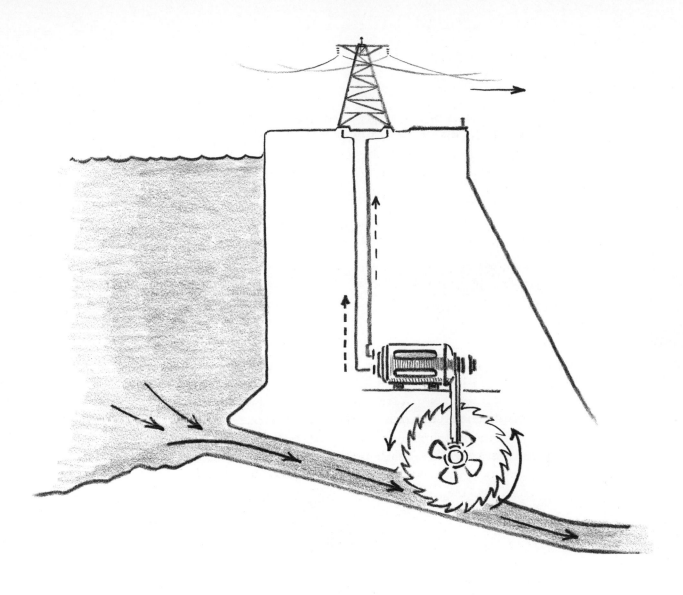

This force of moving water is put into practical use in generating electricity. The turbines that produce electricity in giant electric-power stations are simply larger, stronger, and more efficient "pinwheels."

A dam blocks the flowing water, which then rises and builds up the pressure below. This water under pressure is allowed to rush through pipes to turn the giant wheels of the turbine. The electric generators are then caused to turn, and thus electric current is made to flow in wires.

Dampen the back of your hand with a wet cloth. Blow on your hand. The water evaporates and disappears. At the same time your hand feels cool. The cooling effect of evaporation of the sweat from your body tends to cool you in hot weather. Without this cooling by evaporation people could not live in hot weather.

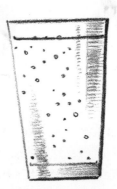

Attach two wires to a dry battery and dip the ends into water to which some vinegar has been added. See the bubbles that form at each wire. The electric current breaks the water down into the materials of which it is made, oxygen and hydrogen, which come out in the form of bubbles.

Let some cold water run into a glass from the faucet. Notice the air bubbles. Let the water stand, and watch the bubbles of dissolved air come out and float to the top. Some of them cling to the sides of the glass. They resemble small soda-water bubbles.

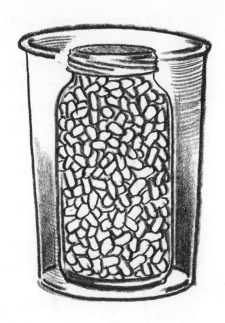

Fill a small glass jar with beans or peas. Then fill it to the brim with water. Cap the jar tightly. Place it in an empty food can. The next day the jar will probably be broken. The water taken in by the beans causes them to expand and break the jar.

Water does not dissolve everything. Add some oil to water. Mix thoroughly. Drops of oil float to the top. Add some detergent. The water is now able to break up the oil drops into tiny particles. That is why we use detergents and soaps to clean greasy objects.

Fill a pitcher with water and pour it onto some dry soil. Watch how the water makes a shallow hole in the ground as the soil is splashed away. Then notice the tiny, muddy "rivers" that carry some of the soil downhill.

During a flood the force of water may be great enough to carry enormous rocks and boulders for miles downstream. Smaller stones, sand and mud are deposited all along the river edge. At last, they reach the ocean and may form mud flats and beaches.

In this way the surface of the earth has been changed from bare rock to sand, mud, and soil. There are other things besides water that have changed the surface of the earth, but water is probably the most important.

The Grand Canyon is a good example of how water can carry away parts of the land. The Colorado River, which flows through the Grand Canyon, has cut its way one mile down into the ground. In some places the Grand Canyon is ten miles wide. Much of the material washed away by the river was carried many miles and deposited in the Gulf of California. Eventually the end of the Gulf got very shallow and the sea water evaporated to form the Imperial Valley—two hundred and forty feet below the level of the sea.

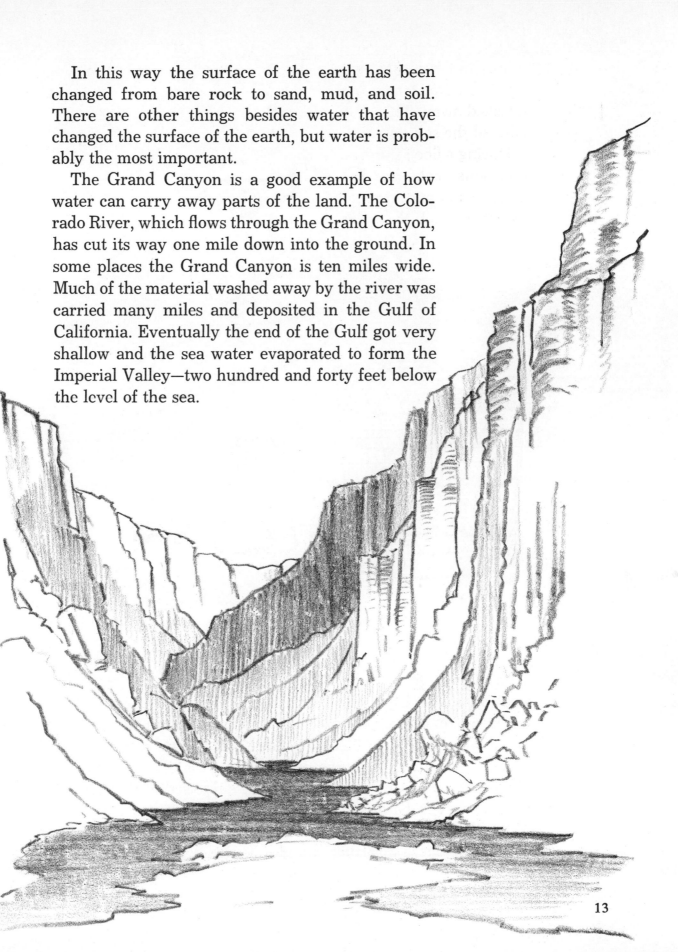

In addition to the solid material carried by water, water may also contain invisible dissolved materials. Put a teaspoonful of salt into a small glass of water. Stir until it dissolves (disappears in the water). Keep dissolving more salt in the same way, a spoonful at a time. Continue until no more dissolves. This solution is said to be saturated. You will be surprised at the amount of salt that can be dissolved before saturation is reached.

Try the same thing with sugar and bicarbonate of soda. Large amounts of these materials can also be dissolved.

A liquid that dissolves a solid is called a solvent. Water is one of the best solvents known. It dissolves more substances and in greater quantities than the vast majority of other liquids. This property of water is most important in industry, where water is usually used to dissolve substances during the making of plastics, paper, chemicals, and many other materials. This property of water is also used to clean machine parts and automobiles. People make use of the dissolving ability of water to wash and bathe. We make many foods by adding water to solids.

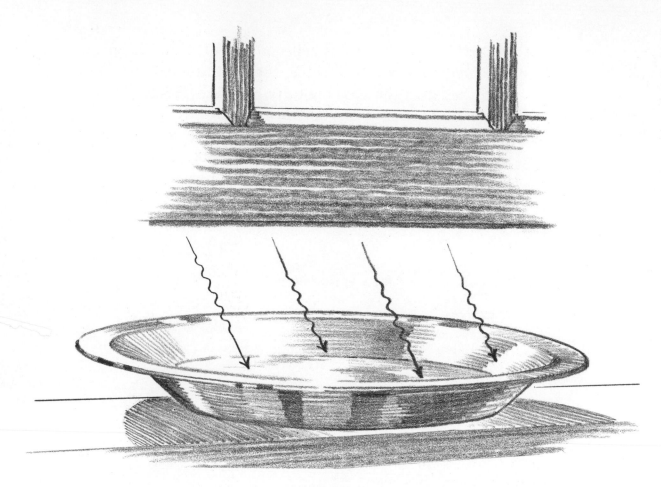

Why is the ocean salty? Rain water trickles through the ground and dissolves some of the solid material, which is then carried down the rivers to the oceans. The addition of these dissolved materials through billions of years has made the ocean very salty.

Pour some of the salty water you made in the previous experiment into an old pie tin or saucepan. Place the pan in the sun or over a radiator and allow the water to evaporate. You will see the salt left in the pan.

In the ocean, dissolved salts are always being added while the water level stays about the same. This means the oceans are slowly becoming saltier as time goes by.

Some of the dissolved minerals in the ocean are now being removed and used. For example, one process for making the metal magnesium starts with a mineral obtained from ocean water. This metal is used to make lightweight ladders, portable furniture, and parts of airplanes.

Water has a great effect on our lives through its ability to absorb large amounts of heat. You can show this effect by boiling some water in a frying pan.

Choose a frying pan with a thick bottom. Put it on the stove. Add a teaspoonful of water. Heat the pan over a gentle flame. In a few moments the small amount of water begins to boil. This tells us that the temperature of the inside of the frying pan has reached the boiling point of water—212 degrees Fahrenheit or 100 degrees centigrade.

Remove the frying pan and let it cool off for several minutes. Then add about a quarter of an inch of water to the pan. Put it back over the same flame. Now the water takes a much longer time to boil than before; in other words, it takes a longer time to reach the boiling point of water.

Careful measurements show that it takes about nine times as much heat to raise a certain amount of water to boiling temperature as it does an equal weight of iron. Therefore water warms up much more slowly than iron.

Let the water boil for a while. Notice how the liquid water boils off in the form of a gas, which we call steam.

The ability of water to take in large amounts of heat without increasing much in temperature explains why you love to go to the ocean or a nearby lake on a hot day. The land warms up much more rapidly than the water of the ocean or lake on a hot summer day. Thus the water remains fairly cool. As a result, the nearby land is kept cool.

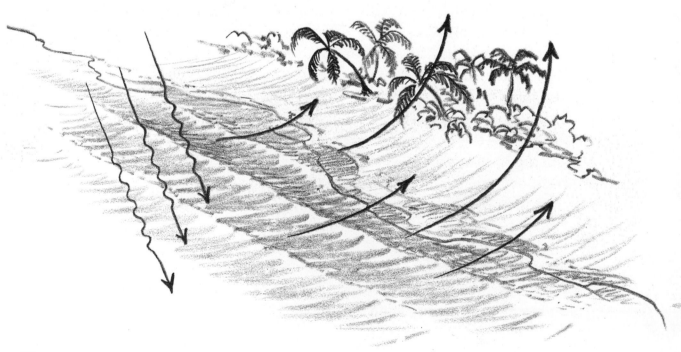

In the winter the water of oceans and lakes cools off more slowly and therefore prevents the surrounding land from getting as cold as it does inland. The climate of continents is changed by this property of water. For example, countries such as England, France, Spain, Italy, and Germany, have temperate climates because the warm Gulf Stream carries a tremendous amount of heat to nearby shores from tropical regions. The winds pick up this heat and carry it inland.

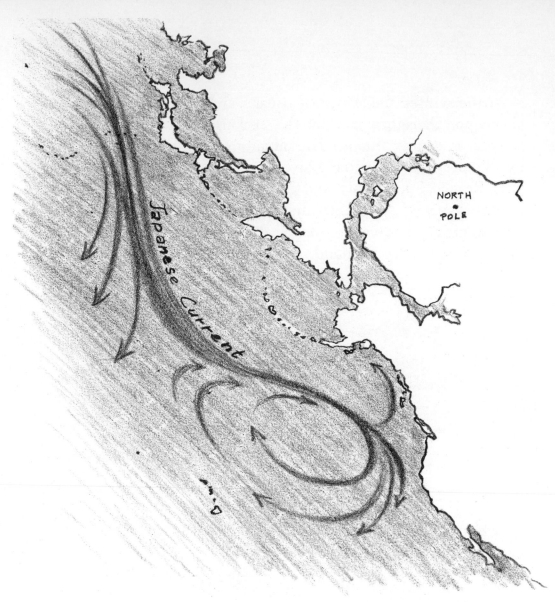

In a similar way, the climate of the western coast of the United States is affected by an ocean current from the coast of Asia.

This Japan Current moves north toward Alaska and then flows south along the West Coast of the United States. Winds blowing from the ocean toward the land carry a great deal of moisture. This moisture is deposited as rain or snow in the mountainous areas from Oregon to California.

In addition, the Japan Current makes the climate of the West Coast rather mild. In summer the water is cooler than the land. In winter it is not as cold. So when the winds blow from the ocean toward land they tend to make the temperature of the land less extreme.

You know that the water of the ocean covers three quarters of the earth's surface. But we also find water in the air and on the land.

Fill a shiny tin can (or a thin glass) with ice cubes. Place the can in a dish. Almost immediately the outside of the can becomes moist. Soon water begins to drip down into the dish to form a tiny pool. You will be surprised at the amount of water that can form in this way. Where did the water come from?

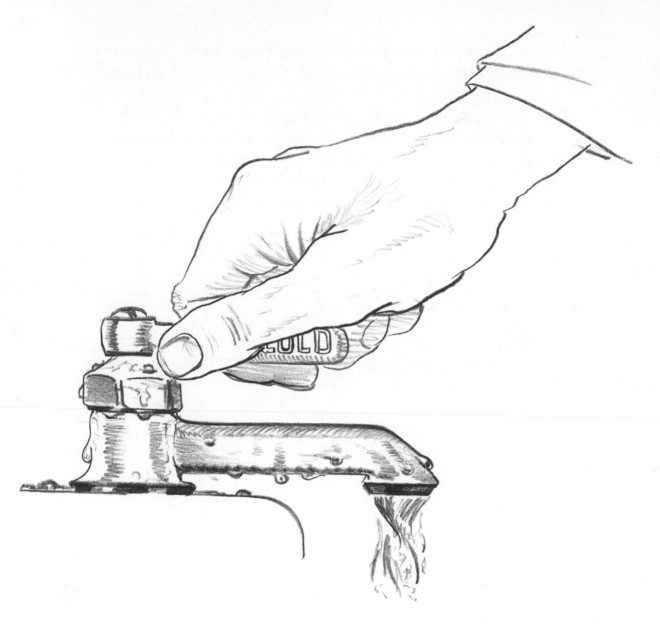

The heat of the sun evaporates the water in oceans, lakes, and rivers, just as the heat in a room evaporates the water in the pie tin that we talked about on page 16—leaving the salt behind. In both cases the water remains in the air as a gas, invisible water vapor. Later, when the air is cooled, the process is reversed, and some of the water comes out of the air in the form of a liquid. That is why water forms on the outside of a cold tin can. Water forms on cold water pipes and on bathroom mirrors in a similar way.

Can you make a cloud? It's easy. Simply breathe out on a cold day. The invisible water vapor in your breath is cooled, condensed, and forms visible droplets of a tiny cloud.

A similar cloud forms when you boil water in a kettle. The invisible steam is cooled, and condenses to form visible water droplets.

Clouds and rain form in a similar way. When air is cooled
enough, the water vapor condenses to form large clouds. If the
process continues, the droplets become large enough to fall. Rain
then gives to plants and animals the water they need for life.

A great deal of water exists in the ground. Try this. Collect some earth from a grassy place, or a forest. Place it in a pot that has been lined with aluminum foil to keep it clean. Heat the pot very gently. You see a mist rising from the soil.

Place the soil in the open, where sunlight can reach it, for a few days. Notice how it becomes powdery and dry as the water evaporates. It is the water in soil that the roots of plants soak up to remain alive.

Much of our water supply comes from wells which we dig in the ground. Below a certain level the empty spaces between the grains of soil are filled with water. This water oozes out of the soil to fill up a well that is dug below the ground.

Place a piece of celery in an empty
jar. The next morning it will be limp
because of the loss of water by evaporation.
Add some water to the jar. The celery
will absorb the water and stiffen up again.

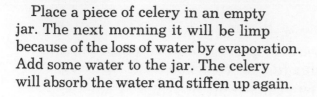

Hold a drinking glass upside down
over the flame of a candle. Don't let
the flame touch the glass, or it may crack.
The candle will soon go out because
you shut off the supply of air.

Notice the band of moisture that
has formed around the inside of the
glass. The water comes from the
burning of the hydrogen in the candle
flame as it combines with oxygen
in the air.

Dissolve salt in half a glass of water
in a pot, until no more can be dissolved.
(See page 14.) Heat the water on the
stove. You will find that a great deal
more salt can now be dissolved.

Heat increases the ability of water
to dissolve materials.

Dry the tip of your tongue with a clean cloth. Place some sugar on the dry spot. You do not taste the sweetness of the sugar. But add a few drops of water to dissolve the sugar. Now you can taste it.

Put two heaping teaspoons of baking powder in a small glass. Fill the glass three quarters full with water, and stir.

The chemicals in the baking powder dissolve in the water and begin to react. Observe the bubbles of carbon dioxide that are formed. These bubbles are what make cakes and biscuits rise and become fluffy.

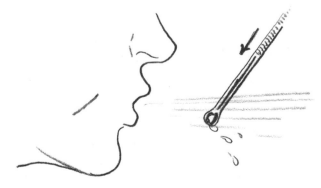

Note the temperature of an ordinary room thermometer. Then add several drops of water to the bulb. Blow gently to evaporate the water and you will see the temperature drop.

This experiment shows that evaporation causes cooling.

Put some dried beans in a small jar. Put some flour or powdered milk in another. Cover both with water. Set them aside for a few days. Notice how the material begins to change. It starts to smell. Mold may form and grow. Froth may develop. Some of the seeds begin to sprout. After a few days the materials begin to rot.

The dry beans and flour have been standing on the shelf for weeks, months, and perhaps years with no noticeable change. But as soon as you add water, life begins. The seeds begin to develop. Bacteria, molds, and many kinds of germs also develop, because now they have the water needed to live. They feed on the moist beans and flour, causing them to rot. But this does not happen if water is missing.

If you plant the beans in moist soil under the proper conditions they will absorb water from the ground and grow into large bean plants.

Why do plants need water? Examine a carrot. It doesn't look as though it has much water. But grate it into a bowl. Squeeze out the water with a lemon squeezer, or with your hands. Where did all the water come from?

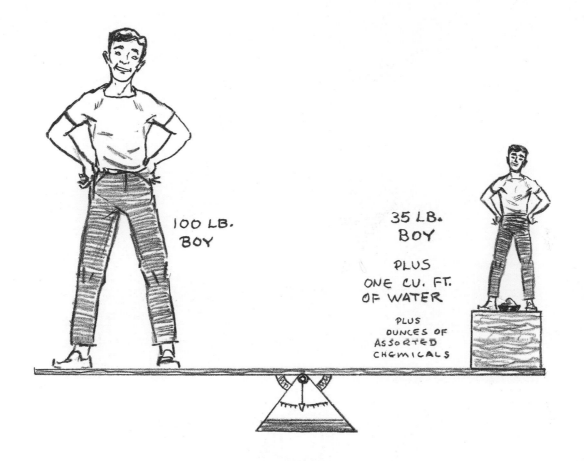

100 LB. BOY

35 LB. BOY

PLUS ONE CU. FT. OF WATER

PLUS OUNCES OF ASSORTED CHEMICALS

About three quarters of the material of living things is water. Not only is the water needed for the actual building of the bodies of living things, but it is also the most important part of their "transportation systems."

Water dissolves the minerals, gases, body chemicals, and wastes and carries them around where needed. Blood does this job in your body. And the water in your blood is what dissolves the other materials and carries them to the different parts of your body, to keep you alive.

Water is so important to life that the living process stops if water is not available. As you know, seeds cannot grow unless they are moist. Even decay (which is actually the growth of special types of animals) is stopped when little or no water is present. Note what kind of foods are kept without cooking, canning, or refrigeration: dried prunes, apricots, raisins, powdered milk, "instant" potatoes, and dry soup mixes. When you add water to them, they resemble the original foods.

Perhaps you realize now how wonderful water is and how important it is to you. Be sure to drink plenty of this "fountain of youth" every day.